The Flowers of My Soul

Poetry and Prose

Lizzie Bair

imprints

The Flowers of My Soul
Copyright © 2022 by Lizzie Bair

Library of Congress Control Number: 2022901672

ISBN: 979-8-9856594-0-5 (Paperback Edition)
ISBN: 979-8-9856594-1-2 (eBook Edition)

Printed in the United States of America

Cover Art: Lizzie Bair
Photo Art: Kevin Bair
Editor: Karie Houle
Creative Design: Kent Jackson
Literary Agent: Donna Jackson

Published by ldk imprints
4671 East Phillips Place
Centennial, CO 80122

This book may be purchased in bulk for educational, business or promotional use. For information please contact your local bookseller or the publisher at www.ldkimprints.com

Dedication

For two of the most amazing human beings on the planet, my best friends Avery and Blake. Thank you for the constant laughs and sticking by me always.

The Flowers of My Soul

If my soul were made up of flowers
I could pick just the right bouquet
The first and easiest
Daisies
Simple as well as intricate
Memories of a life I had
And have now
Second, one of my favorites
A rose
My love for romance
The hopes that I wish for myself
An excitement of butterflies
A red blush in the face
Thirdly, a little darker
An Iris
The purple a foreboding sense of beauty
Something always with me
But a monster uncontrolled no more
Last, my favorite one
A sunflower
Everything important to me
Friends
A second family I get to choose

Contents

Daisies

Simplistic white
Rounded yellow
Smooth
Easy

A center of intricate pattern
Petals that fall off
Victim to the wind
Pelting rain

A flower of many faces
Beautiful in an imperfect
Detailed place of perfection

Similar to life
Problematic
But at the same time
Pretty

Life's Puzzle

One of the earliest activities I can remember doing is a puzzle. It was only three big pieces, but a puzzle nonetheless. I can remember doing 20 pieces, then 100, then 500 then 1,000. It always felt like a breath of fresh air to see the big picture, the product of hard work. But, to me the most important parts are the tiny little pieces. Like snowflakes, no two are the same. They all have their own edges, and curves, and colors. Looking at each individually makes the end product seem all the more special.

I like to think I look at life the same way I look at puzzles. All of the small, special, seemingly insignificant moments have always been my favorites. They say, it is not about the destination but the journey. The little things are the journey, they are the pieces of life's puzzle.

Colors

Gripping the handle I open the door to my second home
Entering the gym
My smile comes to life
Gaze landing on my alternate family
Non - genetic yet just the same
Fingers pinching the strings
A knot unwinds
The mask clatters to the floor
My mask of fake persona
My mask of a flawless life
My mask of black and white
Caging in the vivid colors that make me

We kick box like warriors
Laugh like siblings
A bond so strong
A year away won't smash it apart
No backstabbing, exclusion or whispers in the corner
Just us being teenagers
High on the drug of life
The age-gap between us shrivels to dust
No one cares about anything outside of us
All that matters is we don't have to cower behind our masks

Goodbyes are exchanged
A last conversation
We shove our bright colors tightly inside
Lacing up our masks of nothing
Returning to the plastic personalities that cloak us
We may not be good at acting on Broadway
But we are perfect on the stage of life

They Will Never Know

Searching for money and no one understands
They will never know
What it's like for us
We have to save our loose change
Work for what we want
Anger a constant exhaustion
They will never know
Wishing for a difference
But bad fortune comes our way
They will never know

Sisters

Sisters
Crazy, uncontrollable
Sometimes insufferable
A bit infuriating
Especially when they want a poem
Written only for them

But they are not insufferable all of the time
They bring love
With laughs until it is not physically possible to laugh anymore
They bring hugs
Even when it is not necessary
They bring joy
Their own brand of joy mixed with light and vivid colors
Unique to them

They are not infuriating all the time
They can be anyone's company
On afternoon drives with destination nowhere
In a silent room that somehow doesn't seem so silent anymore
When life feels a little tilted and someone needs to push it back
Making it a little straighter and easier to deal with

Sisters
Infuriating, insufferable
But life without them
Would be just as such
And a whole lot worse

Bruised on the Concrete

Sometimes I get just a little too tired
Tired of living in a world full of
Conflicting opinions
I can see them
Hear them
Around practically every corner I turn

I don't like these opinions
I wish everyone could love everyone
Not let these daggers of seemed truth
Tear into flesh, hearts
Slashing away bonds

Opinions that swirl into a cloud of black
Sucking you in if you're weak
Spitting you out if you
Have no opinions of your own
Bruising your limbs on the concrete
Sparking tears because deep down you know
That there is not much place in a world
For a person without such strong opinions

If I Wanted to Know I Wasn't Pregnant I Would Ask

It truly isn't fair. All they have to navigate is hills and valleys of voice tone, with too much excitement. Learning how to shave their faces, and sprouting up higher and higher, an appetite to feed an army.

What about us? Knives stabbing, paining, clamping and crushing below. A river of red that usually doesn't go where it is supposed to go. Moods that dip to the lowest of lows and soar to the highest of highs. Crying for absolutely no reason and laughing minutes later. Tender chests, and tender hearts. If I wanted to know I wasn't pregnant I would ask, I don't need a whole week to tell me that.

A Musical Life Story

If everyone's life was symbolized by a song, what would yours sound like? Crazy symphonies of silver and brass, mellow strums of strings? I can practically hear my song, find the exact moments in music.

It would start off with trumpets. Cheerful, exciting, fun. Representing a curiosity accustomed to the beginning of life. The beautiful days full of sandboxes, drippy ice cream cones, and the scent of bubbles. When the only monsters were the ones under a bed and the only tears brought on by a scraped knee.

A rising crescendo, breaking into piano emotion. A first taste of life's harsh hand. Mean girls, real mean. The end of a lunch table seat purposely put there to miss everything. Because if you miss everything you are not obligated to take part. The beginnings of a mind loop assumed to be normal, but would normal things be so insufferable? The melody would pick up in spots, but it would drone from ivory keys.

Then happy sounds from flutes, guitars, harmonicas, drums. Sitting within a circle of love. The mythical sounds of opportunity and passion. Sure, the symphony would dip low. Anxiety, heartache, loss, plaguing the sounds. Drawing tears to think of again. But it would swoop into action fast. A music dancers glide to, people fall in love to. A musical story that is still being told, but can only go up from here.

Crying in the Kitchen

Looking through my house I came to a thought
Everyone cries in the kitchen
Yes it's ridiculous and crazy and dumb
But everyone cries in the kitchen

I have cried in the kitchen
Tears fueled by mood swings and teenage heartbreak
Fake friends, more pressing matters
A pandemic that forces you to keep your doors closed
Faces covered, distance made
Causes a lot of meltdowns in the kitchen

My sisters have cried in the kitchen
Little arguments only twins can create
Quarreling and then with red noses and watery eyes
Making up like nothing ever happened
Crying together over sadder moments
But at least they are together, ever bonded
Sitting on wooden stools
Stools forever in the kitchen

My parents have cried in the kitchen
My dad over problems in his head
A chemical imbalance that likes to make the world
Anxious and depressing at the same time
My mom over trying to keep everything together
Taxes and bills
A lost job
The near loss of our home

As surprising as it sounds
Everyone cries in the kitchen

A Storm of COVID-19

I remember when it first happened. It hit like a tsunami of information, and guidelines, and shutting down. I smashed my fists into the wave, wanting to shatter it. See the rules split into fragments. Fragments I could stomp on and never stop. I still wish I could do that. Stomp until my feet bleed and my throat aches, my muscles tired. The fragments disappearing into dust.

I still despise the feeling of a mask on my face. Hiding my smile, all of their smiles. The breathing feels stuffy and hot, but I don't mind that anymore. I just wish I could see their faces. Six feet, six feet, six feet. The sound still rings through my ears, leaving me begging for relief.

We are almost done it is true. But some days it feels like the future is coming in slow, oozing bursts of molasses leaving me in a constant state of waiting. My grief cycle has ended in peaceful acceptance. But at the beginning it was not so simple. I cried a lot. Stuck in my house, walls like a prison. I had lost the constant equilibrium of friends, and school, a lot of my life. After a while I was numb, not happy for the present but sucking in the scarce light of individual days. Soon the sun came back and I was able to sprout and to grow. I became a luscious green, petaled in yellow. Sometimes thunder booms through the air, lightning singes the ground, ice-cold rain pelts holes in my yellow. But after every rainstorm the clouds go away, the air is sweet, and the sky fills with colors, the colors of a rainbow.

Burn Out

Usually I enjoy it
Solving complex constructs of numbers
Calculating chemicals

But right now it's different
Tired and tired and tired
A pool of unmotivation
A constant swim

I try to stay afloat
My head above water
But sometimes it feels as if I'm about to drown

Leaving a House for a Dorm

College is coming closer, and as much as I'm excited, I can feel the sadness following me. Even though I'm almost seventeen I don't think I'm ready to grow up yet. I think I'm going to miss a lot of my life, watching it slowly slip away.

The nights of blankets and blue light. Watching action shows with my dad in his chair, plopped down in the corner. Late night conversations when it felt like my life was crumbling, he always picked me back up. Getting sucked into his world of the past, working in restaurants, biking to country clubs. Heck I'll even miss the times he told me my shirt was too tight, or my shorts were too short. The moments when going on dates became lectures on the male brain, and talking about hot guys was forbidden. In college my dad will be farther away, the safety reins of control will be gone. It's gonna be hard not having my dad around to talk to as much, or to look out for me when my immature brain can't.

The shopping days mixed with coffees and Mexican restaurants. The shows from my mother's time, that still hold up now. Girl talk in the car, giggling over cute boys in the grocery store. When I am away I won't get the daily compliments on my hair or my clothes. Home cooked meals won't be so frequent. A cozy smelling kitchen switched with industrial scented cafeterias. No more weekend grocery trips where I can talk about anything. The responsibility of doing my laundry falls to me now. I am gonna miss my mother, not just for the housework she does for me, but also for the love and support. Showing me how women should be loved and needed, a good example some girls don't have.

The sleepovers in my room. Filled up with candy and popcorn. Watching cheesy romance movies while my sisters laugh, covered with my gray fluffy blanket. Gossip about boys, which celebrity we thought was the cutest. I'm gonna miss leaving behind people I know will support me no matter what I do. I think if I robbed a bank they would bail me out, I mean I would do the same for them. Healing me from yet another boy who let me go to waste, cheering for me with any accomplishment I ever complete. I am gonna miss them, for they were also my best friends, even if I don't say it that much. Not getting to see the last of them growing up everyday is a hard pill to swallow. I'll miss the responsibility of watching over them along with my parents, for in my heart they will always be protected.

A Beautiful World

There once lived a girl. Long blonde hair, eyes hazel-green. Those eyes saw a beautiful world. A world full of kind people. People of help. Voices sounding happy, cheerful, sometimes sparkled with laughter. The girl wasn't naive. She knew about the dark, the corners, the evil places. But for the most part, beauty was in her head and her heart.

Soon the voices and people slunk into the corners. The darkness hiding all of the colors, and the girl left trapped inside. A house once big and cheerful, now a prison. She was stuck behind the bars, wanting to slice them, to melt them, to do anything to escape. But escape was not the dream she had imagined.

The once magnificent world had fallen into disrepair. Smiles, and laughter became muffled and covered by fabric. Fabric the girl hated. Fabric that felt a sick green, of sandpaper and tight. The worst part was, not everyone agreed to the fabric. No matter the science, facts, tragedy, some refused to wear the sick green. No matter how much hate the girl held in her heart towards the fabric, she laced up her smile, stunted her voice, and wore it. She knew the importance, even if she desired for it to disappear.

Her bed became her second home. When the world shuts down the only place to stay attached is the digital realm. Characters in flesh and blood, as well as made from pencil and pen danced across her vision. A temporary distraction from the outside. As always it was never enough. Salty streams broke through the gates, blurring her vision. Streams of grief for what was lost. The doors

16

would soon close again, for longer and longer periods, shutting for acceptance.

But acceptance didn't come easy. The girl's other family of friends were all locked away in their own prisons. The only escape, bright screens of seeing their faces in technology. That wasn't the same. She knew it too. Sometimes it felt like she was the only one having to pretend this all was okay. That this new world was still beautiful, that she would rise above this. Most days were spent playing this game of pretend, because as her mother said, "Fake it till you make it".

Colors splashed in explosions in the summer sky, pencils and notebooks filled shopping carts, summer cooled down to colors on leaves. Education became a whirlwind of stuck in the prison, and being let out into the outside world. The girl got to see her friends more, but not all of them. It was like living on two different planets. Her best friend stuck on the second one. Luckily she was allowed to go to the second planet more often. The bars feeling less restrictive the outside getting its magic back. Celebrating a new 15, eating ice cream, laughing under the stars. Holly, and pine, and cinnamon, and peppermint. A shiny ball being dropped to welcome the new year.

The girl felt happy again. A happy that stayed constant. Constant friends, new and old. Blending in a yellow that she swam in. The yellow keeping her afloat. Her prison gone, freedom flowed through her like wind through a bird's wings in flight. The girl got her own day to celebrate. Not alone like she had feared, but with all of her yellow. Her first yellow, and still the closest yellow.

17

Supportive and funny. The second yellow a source of joy, and laughs, a crutch when things get a little too crazy. The last yellow she wasn't quite sure how she felt about. This yellow was a He. A nice and funny He, different from the rest of his group.

The once sick green now just a bland gray. Not hated but not loved. The world turned beautiful right in front of her eyes. She got to see her yellow everyday, got to go outside and see smiles, got to feel somewhat normal again. A cure to the dark was starting to spread, and everyday a little more light could be seen.

She had the yellow of her friends, the pink of her family, the purple of herself, and the white of the hope that was soon to come. The colors creating a painting of pretty. What a beautiful world it was.

Laying Down in the Grass Right Before Summer

Lying on the grass
Gray puffs in the sky
Music below
A sense of ease
Something I had craved for too long
Peaceful
Happy
A moment in memory

The Top of a Mountain

Covid. A word heard too many times. Too many changes, too many surprises.

Sad at first, heartbroken for all that was gone.

Then nothing at all. Feeling like nothing, living in numb.

Only little bits of happy, excited, love

But those little feelings together make a mountain.

A mountain I climbed on to reach the top.

A top I look out from everyday

Seeing the ugly, the bad

But also the good, the good that keeps on growing.

Angry

Rage dripped in my brain
Acidic and sour
Filling my skull to the brim
Cracking, splintering

It flowed out as tears
Streaks of red and black
Staining my cheeks

Self Growth

It hurt so much. To have to wonder how many more people would walk away, just because I learned what I was worth. My heart was constantly being gripped by the fist of fate, my breathing heaving. IN. OUT. IN. OUT. Anticipating the events of the future. I woke up and mornings felt like laying in wait. Waiting for someone to come out and say they were done. Feeling like eventually they would all fall away. Leaving me in lonesome all because I did something for me. I was an emotional wreck. Angry, oh so very angry. Fists so tight my knuckles popped, screams just on the brink of being released. Then I would collapse into despair. Crying in an ugly fashion. Eyelids puffy, bloodshot trails crisscrossing my eyes. Wondering if this would all blow over. If anything would ever be the same.

I Knew a Stranger

It is truly a strange experience
Seeing someone you knew so well
Looking like a stranger the very next day

Flipping Off the Universe

Sometimes the Universe likes to come in and slap you. Spinning you around in dizzying circles and falling flat, face down, on the street. Your face is marked red by fingerprints of the Divine. The Universe leaves you there, strewn about, face smushed into the ground.

You feel like everything sucks. Days are filtered in brown, nights are drab and gray. You wonder what you could have ever done, to get such a slap. "It hurts!" you curse at the Universe, flicking your middle finger into the air. Glaring straight into the eyes of power.

Then slowly, people bandage you back together. Your best friends listen, wipe the scowls from your face. They hold you up by the back of your shirt if they need to, just to keep you moving on the right track. New friends too. Listening because they care. Listening because they want to. Providing new seats at lunch tables, and long drives in the night. Giving pieces of advice that only the best of people can give. Parents scoop you up from the concrete. Kissing your head and letting you sob. Helping you in any way they possibly can. Sisters laugh along to your stupid jokes, even if they truly are stupid.

Now you can stand on your own. Smiling at the Universe as it smirks. It isn't ready to hit back yet, but it will. You know it will too, but this time you are ready.

Thank You for the Pain

Thank you for the pain
For it gave me thorns
To push up through the soil
Letting me grow further
Higher than you ever could

Crossing the Pandemic Finish Line

Freedom finally
Fresh air through fresh noses
Faces all the way visible
Fearing poison in the air no more
Feeling like the end of one story
Finding the beginning of another

My Roller Coaster

Life is a roller coaster that constantly bombards us with challenge after challenge, but at the end of the ride we arrive faces flushed, hearts beating, adrenaline coursing through our blood streams. We end exhilarated because we conquered our fears and we embraced what makes us human.

These are the things I want to remember. The things that when I go to bed at night, I can fall asleep with a smile on my face because I know the joys of my life, and I can be excited for the future happiness I will soon come to.

I want to remember the laughter of my friends that is completely and utterly uncontrollable. My voice coming out in bursts sandwiched between huge gulps of air, and the loudest, and ugliest, yet most perfect sound of fun. I can see them now. The red faces of my friends, smiles stretched so far across their mouths. Tears in our eyes. Collapsing in a heap of pure exhaustion and content. We can be together and the hours pass in seconds. I could spend days laughing and never tire.

I want to remember my family in our mountain cabin. The silent peaceful nights of sweet air and stars and low lamplight. The whispers that fill the air because everyone is ready for sleep but doesn't want to leave yet. The clinks of game pieces being played, the hollow sound of a chess knight being put into action. My grandma steeping the fresh spiciness of peppermint tea, my grandpa dozing in the corner.

I want to remember the sleepovers with my best friends. The feeling that we could be anything at the earliest hours of the morning. The happy sensation of ice cream, and chips, and candy touching my tongue. The courage we give each other, and the carefreeness. I don't feel like I ever need to worry on these nights, for these nights are what make me feel alive. They make me feel the youth I embody.

I want to remember some of my earliest memories. Being strung on my dad's shoulders and feeling like a powerful mountain. Hugging the soft fur of my sweet dog, and listening to the tinkling of her collar. The dark and spooky nights dressed as a fairy, or a ballerina going door to door for tricks and treats. The magic in the air of Christmas morning hoping Santa came, and seeing nibbles in the cookies we had left out. The soft touch of my mother and father's lips kissing me good night and pulling the covers up over my chin.

I want to remember memories I made on my own. The beautiful dance parties in front of my mirror using my toothbrush as a microphone. The heart pounding adrenaline rush of exercise. My body feeling like it could literally fall apart at any second, but somehow I have the will to keep going. And when I am done I feel high with pride. The secret feeling of waking up at midnight the night before my birthday. Having a celebration to myself in the darkness, encompassed by the hopeful idea of growing up.

When I get to the end of my roller coaster that is what I want to keep in my bank of a mind. The good, not the bad. The memories that shaped me, the things that made me feel alive.

Up In Knots

Sometimes when I am alone in my thoughts I get a little knotted up inside. Ropes and vines. String and wire. Twisting and turning at the thought of what the future might bring.

First, it's excitement. Electricity zipping through the wires. College, dorm rooms. People I can't wait to meet, places I can't wait to go. Boys that will finally notice the spark of love in front of them. Coffee shops, book stores, road trips. A life I have not yet gotten to live because I am not ready to be on my own.

Next comes the hard part. Leaving the people that feel like an extension of myself. I try not to think of this, only focusing on the strings that tie us together. Fate pulled these ones. A string of silver, and gold and bronze. It really stabs at me sometimes. Knowing me and my best friend are going to have to adjust to distance. A distance we had only known when we did not know each other. My other friend, he and I will be thrown apart too. The calling of Broadway and music pulling that string far away.

Vines. The vines are something I never dare to dream. Spiky and easy to get snagged. A future that could be miserable. Failing school, a bad job of only grease and salt. Being alone forever never quite finding my soulmate. Friendships crumbling, passions fumbling. I keep these thoughts guarded knowing full well my whole potential. The vines can stay away in just imagination.

Lastly, the ropes. Strongest because they are of my flesh and blood family. I am going to miss them, and as much as I cannot bring myself to accept it, there are a limited amount of tomorrows for some of the ropes. I soak it all up while I can like a dog in the summer sun. I grit my teeth knowing my dog is one of those ropes. My sisters are going to grow up and I won't be here like I used to be. Moments will still be made but not so fast and not so current. My parents will finally say goodbye as I flap my wings and leave the nest. I understand that it has to happen, but I still feel a resistance to that change, storing up all the joyful moments I can.

The knots inside are a jumbled mess. A mess of what I know will be blood, sweat and tears. But a mess filled with love and opportunity and hugs. A mess I want to dive into because it is a future ever becoming the present, a present I am excited to make my own.

My Heart on a Page

I'm not quite sure how I do it
The words just flow
Out of my fingers like water

Soaking the page in feelings
Dampening it with dreams
These words are my heart
And my soul
Laid out on a page

Wild Flowers

Look at them swaying in the breeze
Each one a different color, texture, shape, and height
Yet they all grow and live and sway in harmony
A perfect mix of together and alone swirled into life

Roses

Fragrant
Sweet
Dreams

Pinks and reds
The color of a heart on fire
Burning from passion
But also from hurt

Have They Forgotten How to Dream?

High School romance blah, blah, blah. They say it's cliche, not worth it at all. The movies are lies, and the books an over exaggerated ideal. At 15 and 16 it is much too dramatic, and chaotic, and a far cry from serious. That's what they say. They say the fire will burn brighter in college when marriage is supposed to be in sight, and growing up has hit the finish line. That is what they say, a web of facts and figures meant to keep us trapped in this chapter of innocence. But sometimes, sometimes I want to see through the web and get a taste of what the movies and the books provide our dreams.

Even if there is pain and cracks on innocent hearts. Even if tears are spilled in such an abundance, filling a salty ocean of sadness, despair, and betrayal. Even if it doesn't work out. Even if the things that fuel my dreams shatter into smithereens of false hope.

Because I dream of sunsets and stars and steaming mugs filled with coffee, of music and laughter and tables for two. I dream of late night drives narrated only by music and the lights from the radio. I dream of those glances in the halls only meant for the other, and red cheeks and pounding hearts just from saying simple words in a simple conversation.

They say you can dream but dreaming isn't everything. Have they forgotten how to dream? The endless desire for hugs and to know someone like the back of your hand? When you commit your life to that of another do you forget how it feels to deeply hope, and get filled to the brim with wonder? Because they grew

34

up already, and took with them the stardust and shining edges of never experiencing a first love.

So I will keep dreaming my stars and sunsets. I will keep hoping for car rides in the night, so that one day, one day I can get my stardust and shining edges of first love.

Butterflies, Butterflies, Butterflies

He makes me feel like a cloud. Light, fluffy, happy. A flawless white in a sea of perfect blue.

Like a firework. Exploding in sparks. Colors upon colors. Excitement and loud.

Like a cup of tea. Steamy, an aroma of comfort and peace. Warm on the inside.

He brings me joy. Joy of bees in spring flowers, birds in the trees.

Brings calm. The eye of a hurricane, everything around destruction but not the center.

Butterflies. In my stomach, in my head, in my heart. Butterflies, butterflies, butterflies.

He

He
Where do I even start?
A boy that makes me crazy
Happy too
Very happy
A special one
Beautiful in the way he simply exists
An amazing and shining and utterly perfect
Boy that I still don't know how to deal with
I still don't know how to stay sane with
I still don't know if I will ever really forget

Control Freak

Today
I ended up
Sitting on my floor
Blanket over my shoulders
Squealing into my hand
Because you showed up on my phone

You are such a control freak sometimes
A control freak because
Most of my emotions
Are somehow controlled by you
And the sad thing is
You have absolutely no idea
I mean how can such a control freak
Not even know how confusing they are?

The sight of your eyes
Of your smile
And crazy hair
Sends my heart into thumps
My face feels a permanent red
When I'm around you
I am not a control freak
For I cannot control the blush
Or the tremors of my heart

When I'm around you
My world is so out of control
I can't seem to get things straight
But I like the crazy curve
For that means you are here
In a world of perfect straight you would be gone
And I would be the one
In a boring state of control

Blissful Feelings

That night I knew
All your bad days
I wanted to sparkle good again
Because that's what you did for me

All They Want is Sex

You ever have a conversation with a friend where you can feel their heart breaking? It's like every word they say crushes their spirit. Smashing down a heart that didn't want to fracture, but knew that it would eventually. She was always the optimist, our sunflower, the one we could call on when we needed light. It just doesn't feel the same to have to be her light. When she crumbles, getting her up is like trying to rebuild a sandcastle swept away by the tide, it will never be built the same.

'All they want is sex' she said. In a way she was right. At the age we are and to be honest at all the ages coming forward all they will want is sex. Why did we have to be built with the body of a temptress but wish for the love a temptress will never receive? It's not fair to us. The movies and the books and the stories don't account for the drugs in the drinks, and the meaningless hookups and the begging for pictures we never wanted to give in the first place. Math, poetry, smiles, and laughs have no place in an animal who only is looking for a short time of pleasure, the mask for a short time of pain.

They might think we are objects. Tossing us around. Shoving in a circle of messed up minds. The media hooks us on grams of romance, but in a world where hearts break from egotistical testosterone, those grams of romance don't give the same high. The same high that they used to when all we wore were princess dresses, dolls in hand, crayons our best writing utensil. They might think we are objects. In certain views they are right, because just like a vase and a glass and a window once we are dropped we will shatter. Our edges ready to draw blood from who let us go. Our hearts caged in the shards of the pain we endured. To say I don't know anyone hurt by them would be a lie. In houses, at school, over the phone we have been damaged. But from the damage come strength and a shield from their constant bullshit.

But what about the good ones? Yes they are there. Not sex crazed lunatics in a pleasurable world. But they can't even see what is right in front of them, and sometimes that hurts more. Venting constantly about the annoying girls they had to let down easy, or the ones who won't take them back, or take them in the first place. Trying and trying and trying, but no matter how much they will never see. See a girl who has a heart open to their everything. She cares too much, feels too much, and when that all goes away still cares and feels. Even if her friends tell her not to.

'All they want is sex' she said. It is true. The love songs don't account for that. And they also don't account for the fact that the good ones are never really good. Never really good because they will never be ours. At least not for now, not for a long, long time. And that is only for the ones who grow up.

The Boy I Don't Like to Write About

I saw you today. The first time since the sun was hot, the grass emerald, and the days long. I don't like to remember you. In my eyes you are a messed up person, and even worse you leave people that way. I usually try not to put you into words. You don't deserve that place. But today, I felt the anger, shame, heartbreak that I did last summer. It frustrates me that you still have such a hold, frustration brought on by the fact that some part of me can't seem to forgive you.

When you walked through that door my stomach dropped. Even though I couldn't see it, I knew that the blood had exited my face. Pale, pale, pale. The words sucked out of my mouth and into the air of quiet. Adrenaline coursed through, my hands began to shake, my heart racing.

The worst part of it all is, I never really dated you. Never really had you, but you, you piece of fool's gold. You really had me thinking that I did. You manipulative, desperate, egotistical, son of a bitch. I still can't quite wrap my head around it. How a single part of you could think what you did to me, and her, and all the other hers was okay. We might look like Barbies in our makeup and our hair, but we are not toys. If you think you can play with us, think again. I hope that your new toy soon finds out for herself what a maniac you are, because every day she spends with you is another day wasted on not good enough.

I try to give everybody the benefit of the doubt. Cut them slack, make excuses. But for you there will never be any. I don't wish you well, because quite frankly you don't come close to deserving it. I hope you have high heel sized dents across your car, hoodies burned to ashes, pictures of you scribbled and slashed to infinity. All things that I never got to do.

You crushed me. I will give you that. Made me feel like somehow it was my fault. But now I see that was never the story. However you want to live your life, go live it. Go be the emotionally abusive man you are becoming, go be the school player that everybody knows you are, because if there is one thing that I am sure of it is this, karma is a bitch and it always knows the best time to strike.

He Said, His She

He said **hi**. We introduced ourselves through the digital pixels of phone screens. Talking, talking, talking, that's all we did for the first few days. Getting a sense of knowing. We had walked the same hallways, gone to the same classrooms, probably passed each other once or twice. But yet, the only interaction we had was electronic.

I guess a pandemic does that to people. Stamps them down until they are just a dot in a house, in a world, in a whirlwind of chaos and nothing at the same time.

He said **talk to you later** and then sent a picture of his face. The common Snap Chat thing to do. We sent faces for weeks on end. Each day I fell harder for the brown eyes and hair, intelligence and wit. Each day I grew more and more upset because she was already enjoying the brown eyes and hair, intelligence and wit. Not just any she, *his she*.

I decided to wait. The universe always has a plan in the end. I wanted my end to be with him. I wanted my end to be my first beginning.

He said I was **cute**. Butterflies raced across my belly, my chest, my heart, reddened my face. I was happy. A semi colon parentheses typed across my phone. One day he broke it off. **I can't do this right now,** he said. **We broke up, I am not over it, I still like someone else.** The butterflies raced back to their shadowy hiding places, the redness leaving tear stained splotches. **Wanna be friends? Yes.** I decided to be the girl best friend because if I couldn't have him, then she should. A new she, an old she, a she he never really had.

It can be hard watching something that passed through your fingers like smoke. Hard to help the person you start to care about care for somebody else. But with everything I do, I did my best.

He said **she didn't want him back.** I offered a virtual hug, the only gift I could give to someone I cared for but couldn't be with in person. Things stayed normal for a while. The constant faces and occasional chatter. School was picking up again. I was starving to see people in person. He decided to stay in his pixel world of peace. I needed a textbook and knew he had one. **I can sell it to you,** he said. The butterflies soared back. A blur of white in the form of a Jeep, a figure taking diligent steps up to meet me. My hair was straightened, hours spent picking an outfit of perfection for minutes of interaction. It felt like I was choking on my words. **Here is your money, this is my dog Gracie.** He rubbed her head lovingly and it felt like this was going to be my beginning.

I was on top of the world. Things felt changed. There was something different in the person I was seeing through my screen. Something brighter and lighter.

He said he **wanted to watch movies with me.** The heart emojis dancing across my eyes. He said I was **cute and pretty.** Those words gave me a warmth I never thought I would feel from a boy. Those words made me feel like I was important. **Good Morning :), Good Night :).** Days of happiness, days of dreaming, days of feeling like this would never end. I was *his she*, or at least . . . I was going to be. I felt it coming. Like a volcano that rumbles underneath the ground, waiting to explode its white hot colors. Red, orange, yellow.

No one ever teaches us how people can play games. The movies always have happy endings, the love songs end with getting the guy and falling head over heels. They never end with one person left with less than they started with. With salty streaks of water, and heaving breaths. I should have known that the volcano would explode, leaving me in ash, in burns, in smoke, in doomsday.

He said **Good Morning :)** and then nothing at all. He shut down everything. **What's wrong? I'm feeling off,** he said. The faces turned to pictures of walls, and ceilings. The hearts to empty space, the words that gave me butterflies to nothing. I wanted to shatter the screen, end the pixels. I wanted to hurt his heart badly. Make him see the girl he toyed. Shout, scream, wail at him until he heard what I was trying to say. Until he felt bad, (and even though I didn't want to admit it), until he came back.

The pain didn't last long. I tossed him away like trash, like a feather, like a broken vase, like a piece of plastic. I got over him. I grew stronger, someone that wouldn't take that from another boy again. The memories still leave a bruise but not a gash.

He said **he got back his old she.** His only real she. He announced it really. He didn't tell me directly because I stopped sending faces. I left him on read for life vowing to NEVER listen to what he said ever again.

His she can have him now. She can deal with his burdens that weigh people down. Stone after stone after stone stacked on top of her until she can barely breathe. She can deal with the mixed signals like a traffic light. Red, green, red, green, red, green, until she wants to scream. He helped me learn I never want someone like him. I will stand tall and not be forced to kneel. I will find a new he eventually but right now I have me.

Just a Crush

Head spinning
Heart pounding
Mind out of control

Questions brimming
Bubbling fizzing
Taking too much of a toll

A deep confusion
An exhausting fate
Something different
But too late

It's the 'What Ifs' that Get Me

If I wasn't so scared of rejection
Terrified of having everything we have
Crumble like a sandcastle two days too old
Then maybe
Just maybe
I would let my heart spill to you
A sweet song of something
A song of the feelings I have for you

Conflicting

Do I tell you?
Do I stay quiet?
So far staying silent hurts
It pains me to imagine what could be
But I would rather swallow the pain
Than have to hear you say those words
Ruining my imagination
Ruining the present
Ruining one of the best things in my life

Sting

Wishing to change feelings
It never works out
Forcing love and affection
Not going to happen
And that kind of pain
It stings the most
And ironically you can't force that sting away

Sometimes Hope is the Worst

Believe me I know it's gonna hurt. Not like a break up, I know that kind of pain leads to undoing. I won't be undone, but I will be wobbly for a while. He was the one thing keeping me balanced, the rope I walk upon not seeming so small and thin. He will still be there but not in the way that I want.

It is going to rip at me. Seeing him on his rope balancing on another girl. A pretty and beautiful and brilliant girl that he gets to love. A girl that isn't me.

I get addicted to my hope. Hope can be the best and most terrible thing at the same time. It holds paints and brushes splotched with yellows and pinks. A bright and colorful future. But behind the hope. Behind the colors, is a dirty and torn canvas. Reality masked by colors. Colors that only covered what was trying to be forgotten.

To him I am just a nose. Known to exist. Seen in the periphery, but not acknowledged. Blocked away because the person it belongs to, doesn't think it is necessary to see.

When the Tears will Come

I don't quite understand why the tears have not fallen, not sloshed down trails of heartache. The emotions are real, I feel them violently. And yet my body is not shaking. It is not screaming, it isn't even shivering in the slightest.

Denial. Can that be the correct answer? Some days it feels like the feelings I wish him to have were there all along and I fall face first into the same quicksand that pulls me back in every time. The voice in the back of my head yelling at me for being gullible enough to slip again. The voice I can hear right now. She is breaking, trying to stay strong. If she breaks all of me will.

Maybe that is when the tears will come.

Not Right in Any Sense of the Word

I am so tired of waiting
For the right person
Right time
Right moment
I don't think I will know anymore
Everytime I think I do
It ends up hurting
Messed up
Not right in any sense of the word

Fish in the Sea

All they say is
Look for more fish in the sea
There are plenty to pick from
But I'm starting to wonder
If maybe I am in
The wrong part of the ocean

A Jungle of Adolescent Boys

Teenage boys are like zoo animals. A variety of beasts, and ugly creatures, and delicate organisms. High school is it's own jungle of boys, and us girls are the ones who take a jungle journey everyday. A jungle so big you could end up in a different place constantly.

I have ended up everywhere. Most of the time I am in the middle of the lush green. Surrounded by vines, with the tallest of trunks connected to a shower of jade leaves. Between the shadows are where the beasts prowl. The lions and tigers and bears too proud for their own good. Sure they might be handsome animals, but I would never go near them. Too much hotheaded pride and ego surrounds them. Up high in the trees are the jewels of birds. Soaring through the clouds never touching the ground. I like these birds, they bring comfort, and friendship, nothing more, nothing less. Beneath me are the slimy snakes and hairy spiders, I never look down and never want to. These creatures can bite you and poison your heart. The best place to be is somewhere hidden in the forest, choosing the right kind of animal to lead you.

I have journeyed underground to mess with the disgusting bugs only once. I never want to do it again. At first it's pretty. The caves sparkling with minerals, the shiny backs of beetles and snake scales enticing. But once you befriend a snake, the happiness is temporary. They twist you and turn you, squeezing everything out of you until you are vulnerable with everything on the table. And once you are ready for them to take a leap of faith into you, and everything you offer, they strike. Teeth into skin, into hearts. Bleeding tears. Poison clouds everything caging off for a while.

That snake changed me, and my life. I soared from the caves and into the sky with the neon of bird feathers. I glided with the kind ones. the amazing ones, the caring ones, the few good ones that didn't deserve to be with the beasts on the ground. I was enveloped in a hug of feathery friendship, and from my place among the clouds and the sun I could see a wise old elephant all by himself. I promised my birds I would be back soon and left for the elephant.

I met the elephant. The wrinkles crinkling it's eyes as it smiled. It made me feel cared for and loved, and wanted. It treated me just as good and maybe better than the birds. We went on many adventures together. Exploring the crystals of waterfalls, and the warm nights full of fireflies and stars. Soft grass and the luminous moon. I loved my elephant more than the birds of the skies. I still do. My elephant is my rock, keeping me alive. He doesn't know just how appreciated he is.

So yes, the jungle of adolescent boys is a hard one to navigate. But once you find the sky and the elephants of your affection, you might just want to stay.

Irises

A dark flower
Purple
Hauntingly elegant

Graceful in its existence
Roots of importance
But ominously so

An Early Rendition of My Anxiety

Buzzing
Pictures flashing
Voices shouting

Buzzing
Down below water
Always drowning

Buzzing
Doubts succumb to worry
Fear smothering

Buzzing
Losing sleep
Tossing, turning

Buzzing
Overwhelming waves
An overwhelmed mind

A Silver Spool of String

Anxiety makes things hard to understand. Stress is something different, everyone feels that way. Everyone gets nervous from time to time, feeling the pressures of the normal world. But not everyone is like me, stressed too much. Stressed to the point where the cup is overflowing past the brim. Engulfing all the light.

Picture it like this. My brain is like a tightly woven spool of perfect silver thread. Every spiral is in place, the center is center, the string is not one step out of bounds. Then something happens. It could be something big, small, or something not important at all. The thread is sliced and slowly, slowly, slowly, starts an unraveled descent. I put it back together. It is not as good as before but still decent. The silver lost a little luster, the spirals a little more loose.

People unravel my string quite a bit. They don't respond right away to a message? Unravel. They make a weird facial expression? Unravel. They seem to act like they don't care about me, even for only a tiny second. Unravel. Things stack up to the stars and my string can stay somewhat together. But at some point things change . . . for the worse.

The pile gets too high and comes down in corners of sharp. They tear and rip my silver string. The silver becomes dull, the string in pieces spirals no more. It feels impossible to put it back to the way it was. After every sharp piece I worry I am changed for the worse. People hate me, I am not trying hard enough, what if, what if, what if? Constant reassurance becomes my thirst. But with that thirst comes the guilt of constantly depending on people. That guilt piles up high to the same stars and falls in sharper edges, dissecting the already diced string.

My head pounds, my thoughts swirling around as the tiny itty-bitty pieces of ugly string. I cannot even recognize my brain when the string is like this. For up to days the string swirls in the darkness and I just get through my routine. Then happiness puts it back together. The silver is fading in, the pieces almost glued, but strong. The spool begins to be spiraled once more. The next few days, the remaining pieces sting my brain from time to time. A past I can't seem to let go. I push through, and at some point the pieces become one tight wound and I am back to the way things always start.

But that is just a metaphor and still cannot explain enough. Imagine this. Imagine feeling like you need to constantly apologize for self assumed mistakes. Imagine always wondering if you are overwhelming your friends. Imagine over thinking every single word in a conversation and how it relates to you. Imagine feeling like you could have done better even if you pushed yourself past the limit. Imagine never being able to let go of the past, the scars still bleeding. Imagine a feeling of worrying even if there is nothing to worry about because peace is so rare. Peace is so incomprehensible there has to be something wrong. Imagine setting the bar so high for yourself that even if you come close to touching it, it will never be enough. Imagine wanting to scream but not knowing what to say. Imagine feeling like your head will explode.

So no, that is not stress. It is not 'just being nervous.' It is not an everyday experience. It is anxiety.

Hey with a Period

What does it mean to say 'hey' with a period?
Are you upset?
Are you mad?
Are you serious?

Or are you just happy and seem really tired?
While I sit here staring
My brain set on fire

But what if you hate me?
What if you care?
What if something I say isn't fair?

So here I am sitting, your words left on read
Wondering if it was something I said

It's been fifteen minutes I'm taking too long
But now I'm worried I'll send something wrong
Hi sounds too casual
Hello seems too easy
You just said hey, and I'm getting queasy

I guess I'll type Hi and hope for the best
And finally put this
Hey period
To Rest

Sometimes the 95 isn't Enough

Sometimes the 95 isn't enough
Because that 5 percent says
I have given up

People will say
You shouldn't be sad
About one little grade
When we all did bad

But after a mistake
My mind likes to think
That if it's not perfect
It doesn't count
And each missed percent
Will eventually amount
To a storm in my head
Where I can't get out

Because I'm stuck here staring
Out a window
Warped by the anxious voices
That force me to listen
To the failures perceived
By my crazy mind
Fixated on that stupid 95

The Monster Under My Bed

Just when I think it's getting easier
The monster comes back
It slaps me in the face
Singeing my skin
A red of pain, of sorrow, of anger

Usually It sleeps under my bed
Resting inside
While I soak in the sun
Eyes wide open
Body in the embrace of heated light
Then it comes in clouds
Gray, sickly dark
Covering my blue sky
My treasured sun

After that it can rain for days
Pelts of water that slap
A residual sting

I wish the monster would stay under my bed
Stay
Stay so I could bask in a forever sun

Lonely

Sometimes I feel all alone in a room full of faces. My messed up head and tormenting thoughts, the only company. Separating me from everyone by what seems like miles.

Things Just Aren't So Simple

My friends call me the hopeless romantic
Constantly infatuated by the movies and the books
Wishing my own story could be just so

In a way I guess I am
I dream of a soulmate
One day being secure in the arms of a permanent other

But with anxiety a dream can slowly become a nightmare
Sometimes I feel false in my friendships
Fearing the imagined inevitable
One day they flee and never return
It scares me to realize that it would be easy
Easy to one day break it off and never look back

It terrifies me to see that it could be the same with a boyfriend
I could drive myself insane with worry
Do they really love me?
Are they going to leave?
What if my anxiety is too much for them?
If I open up will they open with me or shut down and close off?

People will say that when you love someone
The anxiety shouldn't be an issue
But things just aren't so simple
Or at least not simple enough to make sense
In my overly complicated mind

My First Psychologist Experience

I remember the first time I met my psychologist. Such a deep desire, but also a deep fear because it is scary to let someone look into your head. Look into your messed up world and come out with a verdict. Terrifying, but so needed.

Tears were flowing from my eyes like water from the tap. Running, running, leaking, and streaming. Salty streams. My blue-light glasses fogged in a constant steam. A steam of guilt, and anger, and shame, and frustration. Gasping for air. Choking on the words that erupted out of my system. A system so rusted, worn out. Barely getting the gears to turn, aching, paining, hurting just to be normal.

The screen kept freezing. I had to repeat sentences over again. Having the words scratch me on the way up twice sometimes. An anxiety disorder. That's what came out. My messed up world finally had a name. Joy, I felt joy. It seemed an extinct emotion for a while, constantly getting washed away by my own created chaos.

A diagnosis too long left unnamed. Suffering for too long. But at least now it wasn't too late. Even with puffy eyes stinging from the liquid they leaked. Even with a bright red nose and a still heaving chest. I felt a relief I had never imagined to be possible. A relief because the demon in my head finally had a name. If you can say a demon's name they can be defeated. Abolished, every last part of them that tortures you.

My Anxiety Gives Me Music

People want to know what it is like inside my head. My crazy, chaotic, yet beautiful and perfect head. Here it is, a window, a look, a scene from my brain. The edges and curves of the ways that I think and I live and I dream.

Some days it's easy. So easy I almost don't even notice. I don't care how I speak, how I sound, how I act. I do not see the imperfections in every little thing I do. I do not hear the voice in my head telling me to change. Those days are like living in music. The song is the prettiest melody and I am dancing through hours, spinning through seconds. I feel like I am on top of the world and looking at everything underneath me. I can see all of the puzzle pieces exactly where they should be. I feel happy, and excited, and eager, and ready. I am not overshadowed by the spinning scribble of black clouds.

Some days it is manageable. I could be sitting and worrying, but not worrying to the brink of insanity. I say words and immediately wonder if they should be taken back. What if I was mean? What if I said something weird? What do they think of me now? I can shut it down easy. Just take a step back and press the big red button. I can still dance to my music, just every so often the song glitches and I fall off balance, I trip, I crumble, I stay down. But not down for too long. I get back up and dancing to the music. I wonder if my dance steps are too fast, too slow, not moving well enough. On days like these the clouds are in my eyeline. I keep my distance, knowing if I move into one of the clouds it will consume me. It feels like I am constantly on the verge of tears but in control and not crying.

Some days are the worst. The clouds are everywhere, spearing me with harsh rain, bursting with thunder and white-hot lightning. The music is a mess of pitch and shrieks. I am constantly falling, my limbs flailing. I am bruised and scraped and scratched. On days like these it feels like everyone I am close to hates me. I feel alone sometimes like I can never be perfect enough for anyone but my family. It feels like every word I have ever said to my friend, to a boy, was messed up. An awful mix of syllables that morphed things ugly. I feel like I am doing everything wrong and I get consumed by thoughts, and thoughts, and thoughts, and thinking. My chest rubber band tight, my head pounds and I can never focus. The beast of my anxiety pulling the rug out from under me and taking all control. The salty tears of crying are a constant taste in my mouth on these days. My eyes red, my sleep fever dreams.

But here is the thing. All of these days are me. My brain gets to be a part of everything. The good days just get better, the bad days make me stronger. The music can be a symphony of ups and downs, of solo numbers that just don't quite fit but are unique. The clouds can be an angel of white against the bluest sky. I learn to appreciate every amazing moment I have. I am surrounded by people that care about me and put up with my chaos. My anxiety gives me my music, the music I have learned to dance to, the music that will always be my favorite song because it is the song my seed of a soul learned to grow to.

The Problem With My Generation

Sometimes I get so mad at the world
At the people
At the news, and the media

Why do we have to put people in boxes?
Labeling the lids so much
They can't escape them?

I just want to live
And not have to worry
Someone will assume something
Every time I turn a corner

A Hard Pill to Swallow

The words echoed in my head. Pounding my brain. *I'm not getting better.* I truly thought I was. My nails were growing back, the skin on my lips not bitten anymore. But no matter how hard I tried I never could quite win. The monster loomed always. Storm clouds that zapped me with lightning. Stabbing my skin with harsh drops of rain.

It's getting bad again. Whispers of a truth I didn't want to believe, but knew I had to.

A Window, A Chimney, A Vent

The demon was back
Stupid, careless, naive me
Thinking I could fight it all on my own

They were shocked
To know I wasn't doing perfectly fine
Living in a tilted head space
Flitting thoughts flying around
Thoughts I wanted to strangle, stab at, stomp on
If I could rip them out of my brain I would

After it felt as if my eyes had run dry
My heart had cramped it's last cramp
My head spun the last dizzying twirl

We came to a conclusion
A simple one at that
This would not be the end
The demons would one day shrink to dust

A door was open someplace
Or maybe it was a window, a chimney, a vent
But somewhere
Out there
Hope could be found
And that was the greatest gift I could ever ask for

Sunflowers

A creamy, spiky, glowing, tall yellow
Stretching to the sky
Open to the sun

Surrounded by the others of tall
Growing together
Staying together
Content in their shared state of being

Wishes

Dear my past little self,
Your wishes came true.
They are coming,
Your life won't feel so lonely anymore

My Category of Sunshine

It's crazy to me, how one moment can change your whole life. Something so simple, but if it didn't occur, today would be utterly different.

My freshman year I was nervous. A broken shell of too many lost friendships. But that day, that day everything changed. I sat down on concrete, warm from the fading summer sun. I sat down with new people, people I had never known before. Simply because I thought making some school friends would be better than eating alone. And now because of that, I am never alone. I met my sunshine, my yellow, my field of flowers. If it wasn't for that concrete who knows where I would be? I never would have had my first all nighter sleepover. Never walked to get candy at 9 pm, the sun setting, running through sprinklers just because we could. I never would have danced around barefoot in my dress of blue, dancing with the people I now have come to know. Crazy thing that concrete.

Then a yellow square with a white ghost in the middle. This one was a whim and to be honest I had no expectations. I added a boy who the only thing I knew about was his name. Now we are close friends. The first guy to show enough decency and respect to have a friendship with me. If it weren't for that blip of short phone conversations, I am not sure if we would even be friends at all. I would never have gotten to see him act in musicals about history and offices. Never bought Capri Suns to fuel his maybe a little too extreme "addiction." Never have gotten to go over chemistry homework or just have a distraction from other school problems. Never have gotten my white shoes washed after stepping in inches of mud.

It is these small moments I am thankful for the most. These moments may seem insignificant and pointless in the beginning, but in the end they represent some of the most important people in my life.

Buckets

Before high school I didn't really believe in best friends. Everyone before, that filled that place failed to be what I wanted. I gave my all every time. Maybe even too much all. The bucket of water I poured of myself wasn't enough. I had to start scraping paint off the bucket to chip into a pool of effort that was only me.

But now I have a gleaming silver bucket. I have a best friend, and I am a best friend. We get so close that parts of our water spill into the other's bucket, becoming them. Catch phrases, music taste, a certain obsession with animated characters. A system of complete knowing that brings comfort and peace and security. For once in my life I am not worried that it will all disappear in a matter of seconds. For once in my life I know that I have a constant source of joy, and giggles, and stupid stories made together

They say friends are the family you choose. I sure am glad I chose this one.

The Melody of Our Lives

I always thought my voice was too high. Shrieking in excitement a little often, my mother telling me to, "quiet down!" when really all I was doing was talking in my normal way. But, I like my voice. It gives laughter a new window to steal through. It gives my whispers fluffy waves of comfort. It gives my most normal sentences color in the black and white world of living.

Her voice gives the world color too. Pastel yellow like daisies, and then there's the pinkest of roses and the baby blue of wild flowers. Quieter than mine but just as important. Calming as an ocean of salt, and foam, and sand. Weaving in and out through stories of secrets, songs of silliness. This voice is the one I hear the most. It marks my own life story in splotches of memory that could never be forgotten.

His voice is not of flowers but of oak trees standing tall to the blue and clouds. They are the darkest most chocolaty bark showered with emerald layers of leaf. I like to explore that forest often finding myself lost in his tales of everyday life. He can sing, better than I can, better than all of us, me and my friends. The chorus makes the forest brighter, lighting through the emerald. He gives the world a sense of guitar strings and harmony in a single breath of words.

I like all of our voices, for all of our voices make the melody to our lives.

Blue Vase

One day I saw a vase. Pretty on the outside, a caring silhouette. I took the vase home with me, filling it with the flowers of my soul, vulnerability, and self. For a while the vase sparkled in the sun, standing out against my collection. The blue glass meshing well with my yellows and shining reds. I liked how it looked all together, like a family full of new.

As the days went by, the sun went behind the clouds. The blue turned to gray, water pelted my windows, roaring in thunder. My vase didn't have the light shining through. For the yellows and the reds they still looked their very best. Colors so deep it didn't matter what a little light could do, they were still beautiful. But the blue, oh how the blue dimmed.

I couldn't bear to lay my eyes upon it anymore. The flowers inside looked fake, the vase desperate to have something to hold onto. A crowding of the shelf, I had never seemed to notice. I hoped that maybe somehow the vase would fall off and shatter. That way it wouldn't be my responsibility to get rid of it.

A Tiger Ready to Pounce

I usually don't get jealous. Not the jealous type, not a jealous girl, my eyes green but not the jade green of jealousy. But tonight I could practically feel that color. It seeped up through my chest, heating my face a cherry red, I could feel it oozing up my throat, clouding my eyes, lacing my laughter. It makes pinpricks at the back of my eyes, teasing a flow of tears to escape the lids they cower behind.

Isn't it interesting; jealousy? It springs forth like a tiger behind a bush, ready to pounce. Sometimes I wish I were a tiger. Slashing away the vines of envy leaking out of my soul. It really shouldn't be a big deal, and in hindsight probably isn't. But this green, this green is like a film against my face. It changes the once beautiful treasures of my heart into things I want to shatter to stop them from being pretty and innocent.

I feel like my skin is on fire making me want to jump out of it. Like I'm stuck in the mud with only a mind for company. Envy's middle name is worst case scenario. Putting images of all the things you fear, loathe, block away, into your imagination. Jealousy holds the shovel digging the never ending hole I am spiraling into. For what will be left? What will be left when the green filter fades, and I am left with the reality in front of me? What will be left after I have shattered all of my pretty things? Tell me. What will be left?

The People Who Could Have Caught Me

I feel guilty for saying this, but sometimes I wish it could go back to just me and my best friend. These new people can be too much. Sometimes I bask in the much, it makes me feel loved and welcomed, alive in my youth. But other times I want to cower and run away from it. With my best friend we have each other so understood. I never have to worry if my anxiety blurs things, she can always make things clear as a crystal. But these new people are like a smoke machine, blurry days and nights and afternoons on repeat.

She and I are puzzle pieces, just enough of a difference that we can fit together tightly. These new people complete my puzzle, they really do, but I just haven't found where. Sometimes I lose the energy to search. It can be overwhelmingly difficult to add on new people. The monster in my head, sending me into spirals. What if they hate me today? What if they leave? What if I annoy them? I can tell you one thing, it annoys me to the brink of wanting to explode. I can't imagine what it would be like to have a friendship without anxiety.

The anxiety loves jealousy. The dessert to the meal of my crazy. I kick myself for not having enough trust. But when She talks to He, and She talks to She without me, I get a little bit frazzled. Nagging at me to push harder, because He should be talking to me. There has to be a reason when really that's how friendships work, bonds are always going to be there and people talk to everyone, and love and care for each other.

Then the other side. I cannot bear to think of leaving anyone out. Fair, fair, fair, fair screams through my mind. Constantly at the mercy of my kindness, good conscience gone too far. Like micro managing all day, working to the bone to keep everyone satisfied and my relationships not too much or too little, not more or less.

Even though, I love them dearly. They support me when I fall, when I trip and stumble. Sometimes I think ending up smashing my face from falling would be a whole lot easier than dealing with the people who could have caught me.

Pinky Promise

I am forever grateful
I have people that are with me now
Standing by me no matter how much I mess up

I promise to do the same
I pinky promise

Two Treasured Sets of Brown

Brown Eyes. An average color that looks plain, and unexciting to an outsider. At first I was the outsider just barely seeing through the surface. The first important set of brown turned out to be my best friend's. Her eyes matching her wavy hair. They are dark, a lush dark, a quiet dark. Not quite silent, filled only with small whispers. Our eyes compliment each other. The chaotic green finding peace among the serene brown. When she is happy her eyes get sparkly. The sparkles finding my eyes when I am down, or my own created chaos gets to be a little much. Her eyes are like looking into a window of our bond. The countless hours talking about boys. Boys with fluffy hair and abs, with muscles, and everything we could ever dream swirling around in the hopeful pair of brown. The loudness in the ways we have laughed breaking the whispers. I love this set of eyes for they belong to my first best friend, the first person I would really consider family even though we are not each other's blood.

The next pair of brown came suddenly. But I am close to his pair of brown. A boy that turned from a face in a classroom to a face I have laughed and talked and giggled with. They are a dark brown, a supportive brown, an admirable brown. It is so crazy to me that I get to be friends with him, I never would have thought. But the universe works in mysterious ways, giving the most amazing gifts in its bow of mystery. Most of the male tans, coppers, and hazels are quite honestly a little idiotic. A pinch of crazy with a dash of ego, a drop of carelessness. But these eyes hold none of that inside. That's what makes me happy to look into them, knowing I don't have to be scared of being hurt by idiocy.

I have been wronged by sets of mud, and twigs, and chocolate. I have found a temporary comfort with the cinnamons and the coffees of the world. But they are not put on the pedestal of utmost importance in my life. Only these two get to sit there and stay there until they are coated with dust and fading with age. Even if I am long forgotten by these significant figures, their eyes of brown are the ones I will treasure the most.

A Thank You Poem for My Best Friend

This is a thank you poem
For you my best friend
You know who you are

You are a person of beauty
Of light and of love
Of everything I need, of everything I thought I didn't

Thank you for being there
When the Earth got a little too quiet
And a little too crazy from just being still
You kept the movement
Made the quiet seem loud

Thank you for having open ears
Listening to my constant chatter
Of drama that probably doesn't need to be so dramatic
Of stories of crazy that lived to be calm

When I think of the past year
I think of very few good things
My family, my passions, the things that I learned
But I also think of you
Because without our friendship
Who knows where I'd be?

Magic

Being friends with him I learned magic does exist
Because when the curtains open, and the lights dim
It is like he is a wizard up on that stage

No matter the character, the lines, the story
He masters
Every
Single
One

One second he is my best friend
And the next he can be
Any person he wants to

Singing better than most ever could
Causing goosebumps to ripple down our spines
Because he is so skilled at being someone else
It seems so easy
A story book coming to life right in front of our eyes

Applause
Loud and bright
My hands never wanting to stop
Because now I believe in magic

The curtains close
And there he stands right in front of me
Back to his original self
The wizard of the stage

Cruel Fates

I love my friends. More than I ever thought was possible for people I'm not related to. They are the people you could only dream of. The ones in the movies that never seem like they could be real. But they are very real, a real that I appreciate immensely.

What saddens me, is that they never receive what they truly deserve. Sometimes it feels as if the world likes to hurt what makes it magnificent, not squelching out what adds to its troubles. All of them, bruised by harsh boulders of life. I wish I could be their shield everyday, but no matter how hard I try, it is never enough.

There are the cheery ones. Smiles that are captured in almost every single photo I have of us together. But underneath that smile are monsters that I can't even begin to understand. Monsters that are black and red. Monsters that color the world a dreary gray, hopeless things that are hard to eradicate. It pains me to know that they have to fight that battle everyday. Pains me to see such a light have to be squelched by such a dark.

There are the excited ones. So many plans and talents and friends. I am just thankful to be part of their circle. But sometimes I see cracks in that shining exterior. A pressure that only oneself could apply. The overwhelming wave of constantly having something to do, about to tear down their village of a mind. You never realize the struggles of a seemingly perfect person until you get to be let into their life. It is hard to know that even stars like that have to deal with an equally crazy world.

They are my rocks. Kind, kind, very kind. I know them better than most. So I know of their own struggle in the ocean of chaos. A flitting mind of fear. No matter how much I try to calm it, the remedy is still somewhere out there. They are very smart, and intelligent but the high standards they hold turn into jenga blocks. One hit of seemed failure and boom, the whole tower in collapse. It feels like I collapse too, because I know they are brilliant but no matter how smart, they can't seem to see it.

If I could hit the Universe in the face I would. Slap it, kick it, scold it for delivering such cruel fates to such beautiful people. I know, trust me I know. Everybody has their own path, struggles to make them stronger. But sometimes I wish that the Universe could be a little more understanding. Understanding that people already so strong can't be like that all the time. Because those people deserve to catch a break.

That is a Disappointing Thing

She was crying today
Crying an uncontrollable sort of stream
Salty splotches absorbed by a lunch napkin

It felt crushing to me
Crushing because I wanted to help her
But I didn't know the best way to
Didn't know her enough to understand
Exactly what she needed

All of my skills to bring laughter
Bring smiles
Bring stupidity but a well appreciated sort
Disappeared all together
All I was left with was a hug
An 'are you okay?'

To me that wasn't enough
That is a disappointing thing

Stories

When my life is new, fresh, adult, grown. There are some stories I hope to carry with me forever. Share with my new group of happy.

Our blue dresses, and white flowers dotting our hair. Leaving the school dance early because it was painfully loud. Driving and hitting a parked car for the first time.

Laughing our heads off to the most stupid, and wackiest things we could possibly think of. Trying not to choke on candy or spit out water.

Fangirling over random guys we saw at the mall, or the skate park, or the school. Talking over what it would be like to kiss someone. Doing our best to support each other through singledom.

Running through rainy fields with our hair flowing behind us, shrieking with sugar high feelings. Laying down in the parking lot seconds later to stare at the sky.

Staying up for 24 hours because we could. Getting in trouble for shooting each other with scrunchies. Making paper butterflies and spinning around on the metal playground near the house.

Stories of my first best friend.

Driving around in a blue car blasting music. Now a silver one, a stick shift that is still sometimes challenging to drive. Sitting in the back of a van eating lunch together, joking around that we got kidnapped.

Watching performance after performance. Buying bags of cookies, and bouquets of flowers. Rewriting cards that got lost only to turn up later. Gifting boxes of Capri Suns because we both knew a smile was needed.

Working through chemistry problems that probably take a little bit longer than they should. We talk and laugh all the way through the night.

Motivating a climb to the top of the playground, that never seemed to work. No matter how hard we both tried to get me up there.

Keeping each other company while working through homework, and playing the guitar and spray painting shirts silver for a Halloween costume. Wondering how in the world we got close so fast, but never once regretting it.

Stories of my second best friend.

Sunlight and Stars

I'm not sure how much they know
That even on my darkest most dreadful days
They give me sunlight and stars
Just by being themselves

A Night to Remember

It was a sign I think
Skies from light gray
Fading to pink
Then an orange of peaches

A distance of mountain ridges
Ombre in hues of indigo and blue

The sun a ball of cheerful fire
Deeper colors than the peach of the sky

That night I felt a weight lift
Shoulders finally able to breath
The Universe knew what to do
It always did
I had just lost a little faith is all

A Letter to the Reader

Dear Reader,

Thank you for giving this teenage girl a place to share her passions and her feelings. Thank you for giving her words a chance.

Hopefully you found comfort in knowing that you are not alone. We are different, everyone is. Everyone struggles, whether it be with love, mental health or friendships. Life can be hard.

I hope this book brought you joy and gave you the knowledge that no matter how hard life seems there really is something magnificent just around the corner. That is the beauty of the world we live in. We can always find comfort after a troublesome present.

Reader, my flowers and I wish you well and hope you can learn to love your flowers, too, each and everyone.

Acknowledgements

First, I would like to thank…my Grandma for being my agent and the mastermind in the publishing process, my Grandpa for helping me illustrate my book and for working behind the scenes to make it happen and my cousin, Karie, for being a fabulous editor and assisting me from the very beginning.

I would like to thank my parents for supporting my dreams and listening to me read countless poems and my two sisters who provided so much inspiration. They are always there for me, giving some of the most amazing daisies ever. I am very thankful for one of the best families in the world. This book would not have been possible if not for all of them.

Next, thank you to Tara, Sara, Lexi, Emma, Alex and the entire ThunderRidge High School Peer Counseling Department for being some of the best sources of support and inspiration. They are truly wonderful people that I am glad to have met.

Finally, I would like to acknowledge all of the relationships I have had throughout my life. They have helped make this book a reality, shaped me in unimaginable ways and I am grateful for the impact they have made on my journey.